Contents

Further Education and Adult Learning

A NIACE policy discussion paper

Colin Flint

promoting adult learning

promoting adult learning

© 2004 National Institute of Adult Continuing Education
(England and Wales)

21 De Montfort Street
Leicester
LE1 7GE

Company registration no. 2603322
Charity registration no. 1002775

NIACE has a broad remit to promote lifelong learning opportunities for adults. NIACE works to
develop increased participation in education and training, particularly for those who do not have
easy access because of class, gender, age, race, language and culture, learning difficulties or
disabilities, or insufficient financial resources.

You can find NIACE online at www.niace.org.uk

Cataloguing in Publication Data
A CIP record of this title is available from the British Library

ISBN 1 86201 206 7

Designed and typeset by Creative
Printed and bound in the UK by Latimer Trend

Foreword

NIACE has an overall remit to promote the interests of adult learners wherever they learn, and to support those who make provision for them. It is a charity and company, and its members are drawn from further and higher education, voluntary and local authority sectors, from broadcasters, trades unions, industry, the health sector, the military and from individuals committed to adult learning. NIACE's key policy priority is to secure more and different opportunities for adult learners, and in particular for those who have benefited least from other educational offers.

NIACE undertakes its work in a variety of ways – through advocacy, research and development, conference and training programmes, campaigns to promote learning, and through publication.

As a significant publisher in the field of adult learning, NIACE publishes a range of materials, without endorsing formally their views. In addition the Institute publishes policy papers of its own. These take two forms. The first are formal statements of NIACE policy, endorsed by its Policy Committee acting on behalf of NIACE's Board, often produced in response to current public debates. The second are policy discussion papers – produced to sharpen debate in areas the Institute judges to be of importance. These papers are debated by the NIACE Policy Committee, and redrafted in light of those discussions. They carry broad endorsement from the Institute as significant contributions to debate, though the detailed judgements are those of their authors. *Further Education and Adult Learning* is a policy discussion paper.

There can be no more important area of focus for NIACE than provision for adult learners in further education. Since over 80 per cent of students enrolled in colleges of further education are over the age of 19, and over 77 per cent are over 21, it is clear that the FE college sector *is* a sector for adult learners and not just young adults, and should be perceived to be so.

Colin Flint was commissioned to write a policy discussion paper drawing on his experience as a college principal. As a member of the Executive Committee for ten years he is also well acquainted with the range and relevance of our work, and since the work was commissioned Colin has joined NIACE as Associate Director for Further Education. He, like us, is concerned that recent policy objectives placing heavy emphasis on the colleges' role in 14-19 education, with the consequent financial priorities, may be putting some of their equally important work with adults at risk.

The paper reviews the current position of the FE sector and some of its recent history, the impact of current policies of Government and the Department for Education and Skills, and seeks to remind FE of the importance of the pluralities of its mission and its role. It concludes with a number of key policy recommendations and identifies who should take responsibility in their realisation.

NIACE commends and supports the paper and its conclusions and will work towards their implementation.

Alan Tuckett
Director

Further Education: recent history

"We found that while recent policy acknowledges both the economic and social benefits of learning, it does not recognise sufficiently their interdependence. The result is that priority in further education is given to economic goals at the expense of learning for life".
Learning Works, Helena Kennedy (FEFC, 1997)

Six years on, under a new Government and a new funding (and planning) agency, and after considerable national soul-searching about our education system, and scores of new directives and consultation papers and policies, much the same might still be said. It is inevitable that Governments will place their emphasis on economic performance, but the issue of interdependence is still not sufficiently understood. It is there in much of the rhetoric, increasingly it is there in new policy, but it has not been evident in much of the implementation.

Kennedy presented a vision, a goal, of a 'self-perpetuating Learning Society', and saw a means of bringing it closer:

"the key to developing a society of learners is the recognition of a universal entitlement for all to acquire a level 3 qualification, including appropriate key skills."

Six years after the election of a Government which proclaimed a policy of 'education, education, education', our ambitions are somewhat more modest.

One of the shifts that has taken place since Kennedy wrote is a changed view of the further education sector. It has always been a shadowy part of the system: a rose (at its best) that blushed largely unseen, but Incorporation and the creation for the first time of a national body (the Further Education Funding Council) and a national sector appeared to offer a new beginning. Unrealistic demands and funding restrictions by the then Government, well-publicised failures in certain parts of the system – largely occasioned by ambitious attempts to exploit the newly-devised funding methodology – plus the unwillingness at the time to face the issues of inappropriate qualifications and curriculum structures, meant that the sunlit uplands soon disappeared from view. Real growth stubbornly refused to materialise, and the chimera of franchising was exposed for the monster that it had become.

Life grew hard. The inspection regime became more punitive (and much more politically-driven) and 'education, education, education' was replaced by 'audit, audit, audit'. Select committees met. Colleges lost sight of the curriculum and their capacity to influence it, not helped by turmoil and failings in their own national body. From the position where 'further education' looked capable of entering into its birthright, and becoming pivotal in the education system, linking schools and HE, education and business, we reached the position where the words were excised from educational language. FEFC disappeared, so did some colleges and a great many Principals, and the Learning and Skills sector was born.

The Blunkett Letter

David Blunkett's Remit Letter to the Learning and Skills Council in November 2000, still a key reference document, expressed a vision as inspirational as that which informs *Learning Works*. Two central paragraphs bear repeating here:

"We have a great tradition of learning in this country, including the great heritage of adult and community education which developed in the 19thC, when the pioneering efforts of the community movements helped many men and women to improve their lives through the power of learning. We must build on this tradition to restore a culture of commitment to learning. Such a culture cannot be created by organisational change, but it can be fostered and supported by working in partnership with others.

Learning has a major contribution to play in sustaining a civilised and cohesive society, and underpins the Government's objectives for the renewal of deprived neighbourhoods. Learning encourages people to develop as active citizens and to play a full part in their local community. It strengthens families, builds stronger neighbourhoods, helps older people to stay healthy and active, and encourages independence for all by opening up new opportunities – including the chance to explore art, music and literature. And what was available only to the few can, in this new millennium, be enjoyed and taken advantage of by the many".

We were all heartened to see the commitment implicit in this, and it would be unfair to argue that the Department for Education and Skills has deviated significantly from the agenda it set out. Later policy documents and initiatives have carried forward the central thrust, in the 14-19 curriculum, the Basic Skills actions, the HE White Paper, the Skills Agenda, with 'Success for All' describing the overall strategy. If the vision were to be realised, whatever our reservations about some of the detail, then the transformation of the education system into one much more fit for purpose will have been achieved. It would be fit for all the people, not the minority which it was designed to serve. It is, of course, another Forth Bridge job: the objectives will move on, the exigencies will change, but we would have removed or modified some of the major structural weaknesses which have beset British education for generations. We would be much closer to a socially cohesive society, we would have greatly strengthened the capacity of the economy, and we would be offering opportunity to millions who have been failed by past arrangements.

Until we have actually seen it all work, however, the problems remain. We are still a very long way from Kennedy's self-perpetuating learning society, and there are dangers that for many learners things will become worse rather than better. As the Skills Strategy focuses its direction and resources on adults without a level 2 qualification and on level 3 only in sectors of the economy identified as 'priority' – and clearly these objectives have to be supported – then other adult learning is likely to suffer. Free tuition to boost adult skills may be a necessary measure, but the resources will be redirected, not additional. If the primary function of colleges is to be seen as a cost-effective means of raising the school-leaving age and providing a relevant curriculum for large numbers of 14-19-year-olds, and resources are so targeted, then further education will change fewer lives in older generations. If colleges have to rewrite their missions in order to be seen to be delivering specific Government policies, they – or some of them – will reduce their commitment to, and capacity for, doing equally valuable work with adult learners. Such an outcome would undermine not only the Kennedy and Blunkett visions, but also much of the long-term objectives of the Government's strategy.

FE and adult learners

In the academic year 2001/2002, there were 4,151,600 students enrolled in colleges of further education. Of these, 3,375,000 were over the age of 19, and 3,179,000 of the total were studying part-time.

Most students are funded through the Learning and Skills Council, a total of 3,840,000. Of these, 3,236,000 were over 19. Of these students funded by LSC, 92.3 per cent were studying in general further education colleges with the remainder (7.7 per cent) in sixth form colleges or other specialist provision. Of the full number (4,151,600) 93.6 per cent were in general FE. As nearly as can be calculated from LSC statistics (non-LSC funded students are not shown in narrower age bands) approximately 800,000 students in 2001/2002 were under the age of 21, with 3.22 million over that age. (Of all enrolments, 59 per cent were women.)

Over 80 per cent of all student enrolments in all colleges are over the age of 19: over 77 per cent are over the age of 21. Furthermore, between 11 per cent and 12 per cent of all those studying in FE are following a course which is classified as higher education (i.e. level 4 or 5). A very large majority of these are over the age of 25. The colleges – general further education colleges – are unarguably part of the post-compulsory education system: FE is overwhelmingly an adult and part-time service; adult education is the core work of colleges.

These are facts, but they need to be emphasised, because it is by no means clear that this image is the one that is strongest in the minds of the public at large, nor of at least some of those who work in the service, and some of those who work in Government.

The purpose of this paper is to serve as a reminder of the fundamental importance of FE colleges to the achievement of a learning society, for the creation of a lifelong learning culture, and to the realisation of some of the key aspirations for the education service as a whole. There is no question that the colleges have a vital part to play with regard to specific targets – for example the delivery of a curriculum for those aged 14-19 which is relevant to the needs of the economy and to individual students. However, to limit that role, to give pre-eminence in the resourcing and strategic planning of colleges to tasks which a properly-planned secondary system would deliver, is to put at risk the richness and diversity which is the true strength of good FE colleges.

The growth of full-time provision

The rapid growth of full-time courses in FE is a relatively recent phenomenon. Full-time provision in colleges – almost invariably 'technical' colleges – grew relatively slowly in the 1950s and 1960s, as industrial needs, individual prosperity and economic patterns began to change. Many local education authorities had established their own colleges (which was not a requirement on them), some developing out of older mechanics institutes, some out of technical schools. Bilateral schools, technical high schools, were one of the innovative and necessary proposals of the 1944 Act, but were not widely adopted. In fact there was not then (most certainly not before and arguably not since) a co-ordinated or concerted effort to see the kinds of improvement in vocational educational opportunity that should have been regarded as essential, both for school-leavers and for older workers. Neither in 1938, after the publication of the Spens Report, written in the face of a second catastrophic world war, nor in 1944 when some of the lessons of that war had surely been learned and a new framework for education was created, did Britain undertake the kind of programmes for the advancement of its technical education system that it needed. There is a poignant passage in the Spens Report on secondary education which has echoed down the ages:

> "the most striking feature [of the new secondary schools] was their marked disinclination to deviate to any considerable extent from the main lines of the traditional grammar school curriculum… Although 85 per cent of pupils did not remain at school beyond 15, the curriculum was largely planned in the interests of those who intended to go to university."

Then and subsequently we held on to the essential structures and patterns of an elitist education system. We have gone on defining the problem (the Crowther Report, Newsome, Dearing *et al*) without taking the steps necessary to remove it. Our 'academic' stream remains the most specialised and narrow of any in the industrialised world. We have tinkered, but not reformed.

Partly in consequence, the demand for full-time courses in FE (for example in Art and Design – located nowhere else in the system – and secretarial studies, and other vocational and pre-employment courses) developed in the colleges alongside the staple of day-release courses from industry and the rich provision of non-vocational (and vocational) evening classes, and increasingly daytime classes, for adults.

Colleges grew through the 1960s and 1970s. More of them were created: almost all of them expanded and diversified. The biggest impetus to growth was the raising of the school leaving age in 1972, stimulating demand for qualifications. But colleges remained a rather unloved and untended part of the educational garden. They grew like vegetables which in the 17th century and before were thought to have only two powers, those of growth and reproduction. By and large, they looked after themselves. There were few horticultural experiments undertaken, except those initiated in the colleges themselves: they were not much nurtured. There were other plants, in other parts of the garden, which were much more prominent and which received much more attention, the fruits of which were much more highly prized. But colleges had become an increasingly important part of the provision for school-leavers, especially those disaffected by their experience of school.

To state the obvious, colleges are part of the state system, and there can be no doubt that they are properly required to play their part in looking for solutions to the acute problems of that system. Equally there is not doubt that the present Government has placed much greater emphasis and urgency than its predecessor on putting right the deficiencies of the past. Britain has been both complacent and pusillanimous about the reform of education: there is now a greater recognition that it cannot afford to be so in the future, and that the work of the FE sector, or the learning and skills sector as we now must call it, is an essential component of a reformed system. But in asking it to deliver in one of its many functions, we must not eviscerate the rest.

Attainment at 16 is a key determinant of future prospects, and we are too well aware of current wastage levels at 16 or 17, where our national performance is amongst the worst in OECD countries. The emphasis on improvements in the outcomes from secondary education is right, and the 14-19 reforms will be achieved quicker and more cost-effectively if FE is working closely and co-operatively with schools. But it must not be at the expense of the work that colleges do with the disadvantaged and with mature students. Social inclusion means everyone, and all of those who have been failed by our education system in the past need the best resources if FE if they are to find their way back.

Helena Kennedy's *Learning Works*, in this author's opinion the best book ever written about further education, is worth quoting again at this point:

> "It is further education which has invariably given second chances to those who were forced by necessity to make unfulfilling choices. It said 'try again' to those who had been labelled as failures and who had decided education was not for the likes of them. It is here, above all, that opportunities have been provided for those caught in the cycle of low-skilled jobs and unemployment who want to better themselves: here, that so many can retrain; here, that there is work with refugees and members of immigrant groups to acquire English language skills or with ex-offenders to facilitate rehabilitation, or with underachievers to fulfil their potential. It is because the achievements in further education are so rarely lauded that we have failed to recognise further education's potential as a vital engine not only of economic renewal but of social cohesion."

All still true, all still important.

Government priorities

If we accept that the Government's overriding objectives are to promote social inclusion, equality of opportunity, and economic prosperity, and if it is further agreed that we have a lot of ground to make up in order to achieve these goals, it is obvious that priorities have to be set. Broadly, as defined in PSA/DfES targets, these are:

- to increase enrolment in HE to 50 per cent of those aged 18-30

- to widen participation in HE

- to reduce non-completion rates in FE

- to improve adult basic skills

- to increase the percentage of 18-19-year-olds with level 2 qualifications.

The FE sector (or the Learning and Skills sector) is essential to all of these. The link between all of these objectives and the work of the general FE college ought by now to be well understood, but cannot be taken for granted. The list in itself argues for new models of association between FE and HE institutions – of which more later – and for strategies between and across the two sectors. It may well be said to argue also for regional approaches to planning, in which the Regional Development Agencies, the local Learning and Skills Councils and the Higher Education Funding Council work closely together. There are compelling structural reasons for such a development in due course.

The priorities also argue for a very clear understanding that the work of colleges with adults is at least of equal importance with improving attainment levels of school leavers. Both are vital, both need equal emphasis, and Government, LSC and college strategies need to be conceived and planned accordingly. Funding, target setting, partnerships with HE as well as with schools, qualification structures, skills development, all need to reflect such a vision.

Funding FE

Most colleges are dependent on Government sources for between 70 and 80 per cent of their total funding. Typically, something over 65 per cent will come through LSC to fund the agreed programme of 'ordinary' FE; many larger colleges receive around 10 per cent from HEFCE for their higher education work; there are usually smaller additional funds for specific projects again channelled through the local LSC. Other income is made up of student fees, which of course the majority of FE students have always had to pay, international work – a significant earner for the minority of colleges which have established themselves in this field – and direct earnings from industry for full-cost training. The dependency on LSC funds has increased, as this quantum now includes funds previously channelled through the Training and Enterprise Councils, and from the European Social Fund.

The Learning and Skills Council is by far the biggest educational 'quango', with a current annual grant of the order of £8 billion. It follows that the view of Government and the Treasury of the sector is critical, and that performance is under close scrutiny.

The performance of the nation, as discussed in more detail elsewhere, does not compare favourably with competitors, and the number of qualifications in the workforce is a key indicator. (See section on OECD research.) Qualifications are quantifiable, easy to count: they are a crude measure of value for money. They are also one of the generic tools used by OECD in its comparative studies.

This paper has no argument with the obvious truth that there is a serious national problem with Basic Skills (or more properly with acceptable levels of literacy and numeracy), nor with the need to ensure that more young people leave full-time education and training with a sound foundation, and reach national benchmarks, nor with the clear need to reduce the skills deficit in the workforce. However, the vocational qualifications system within which colleges (and learners) have had to work is not fit for purpose. Measuring achievements of learners solely by the number of (whole) qualifications achieved penalises learners and providers and distorts funding. The problems with the existing qualifications system are dealt with at greater length elsewhere – this subject needs a chapter of its own. Suffice to say here that the secondary schools curriculum does not work effectively for half the young people in the system, that current qualifications do not meet the needs of industry, and that it is still the case for too many that – to paraphrase Helena Kennedy – if at first you fail ... you fail.

Qualifications undoubtedly are or can become a motivating factor for many adults if they are perceived as relevant and useful in their lives and careers. They are a source of great pride and satisfaction, whether at entry or degree level, but it is a great deal harder to persuade adults who have gained little or no benefit from their experience of the education system to go on trying than it is those who have been fortunate enough to proceed smoothly alone the qualifications highway. There has been too little recognition of the very considerable efforts that have been made by educators in further and adult education to reach the former. Clearly the widening participation funding has been valuable, but it needed to be accompanied by a more sensitive, and longer term, strategy and approach to the funding of the work.

A basic principle should be that access to recognition of achievement should be available to all, and encouraged especially for those without qualifications. A funding methodology needs to be sensitive and supple enough to be a tool for development as well as a reassurance to the Treasury. It needs to be flexible enough to enable a longer view of skills development: with many learners it may be the third course of study which is measurable in current DfES targets. If we are going to be wholly serious about the creation of a learning society, we should be seeking to fund learning less mechanistically, and ensuring that those in most need receive most help. A concept of entitlement to at least level 2 would be socially just and educationally progressive. It begs the ongoing question of measurement, but if we were to establish the principle, we could surely create the methods. And targets of this kind clearly contribute to social inclusion as well as raised achievement. They become enablers in themselves, not inhibitors.

The funding system devised by FEFC after Incorporation was fair, transparent, even elegant: it was the first time there had been a national system for funding designated further education. But over time it grew to be impossibly complex and increasingly hard to regulate. Franchising became a disaster, though the intentions behind it were sound enough, and the scams discredited it. Auditing arrangements became increasingly punitive. The National Audit Office trusts auditors more than it does educators, despite some spectacular auditing failures. The target/audit regimes under which colleges have operated have worked against the interests of far too many actual and potential learners.

Schedule 2 and beyond

Schedule 2, separating vocational from non-vocational programmes, disqualified much adult learning from funding support, though paradoxically resulted in an increase in overall volumes of adults in FE. This was more to do with the unevenness of previous LEA support than with any inherent virtue in the Schedule 2 thinking, which was posited upon essentially unhelpful notions about the purposes of adult learning. Good educational practice also played its part: growth was also due to the creativity of good adult educators using Open College Network learner-centred accreditation models in order to qualify for funding. In any event Schedule 2, much criticised, disappeared with the Learning and Skills Act (2000) and was replaced, through Sections 96 and 97, with a similar distinction between provision leading to approved qualifications, and 'other' provision. This has introduced a whole new area of uncertainty and potential threat to much work with adults. In 2001/2002, the total of adult students studying in FE colleges on programmes designated as 'other' was 2,020,000, of which 1,096,400 were studying at level 1, 646,700 at level 2, and 273,900 at level 3. The last figure does not include Access to HE courses, also categorised as 'other'.

It is surely a clear indicator of an incomplete and conceptually flawed system if it is unable to categorise most of the work it is funding. The LSC guidance has been that such provision ('other') must not grow at the expense of that which is listed in Sections 96/97, and in some local LSC offices this has been translated into a reluctance to fund non-qualification courses in colleges, putting at serious risk much effective and high quality work, particularly with adults. Attempting to force adults into qualifications which on all the evidence are not what they want and which do not meet their needs, and which even DfES has recognised as insufficiently responsive might be thought to be somewhat perverse. This has been a recurring problem; a failure to recognise – or to fund – this provision, much of which is vital for the re-engagement, or 'pull through' of learners. To put it at its most delicate, it is not a good idea to leave such decisions at the whim of local LSC staff. Under present arrangements, there is real risk that provision for adult learners will be reduced and that demand will not be met.

There is also a danger that the offer and choice for adults will diminish. Colleges will have completed their planning for next year, and the majority will have taken a finance-driven and cautious stance. The announcement of a pilot scheme which should help the continual development of Open College Network and Access to HE provision for adults may have come too late, much though it is to be welcomed.

There is some hope. We appear to be embarked on a fundamental recasting of vocational qualifications which will be credit- and unit-based, and there is recognition that we need systems that fund learners, not institutions. The 'fund the plan' proposals look like an attempt at a new and more appropriated strategy, with the introduction of the plan-led three-year system imminent (2003/2004) and the phasing-in of a more sympathetic approach to budgetary adjustment, in which the threat of in-year reductions will be removed.

However, the review of the funding of adult learning, as part of the work on the skills strategy, is likely to mean that 'non-target' adults will be required to pay more, which will inevitably reduce participation. Less provision is likely to result. The absence of a replacement for the Individual Learning Account scheme is also depressing, even though that scheme was used much more by the educational 'haves' than the 'have-nots'. The 'phased and planned' introduction of new funding arrangements for adult learning will rely heavily on local LSC planning processes: experience suggests that the results will be variable and not always linked to local context and need.

There is need more than ever to do all that can be done to remind all those engaged in the formulation and implementation of policy, including those working in colleges, that adult education is not a luxury, not an add-on when the other targets are achieved, but a vital part of the nation's future. There is danger of forgetting, or merely paying lip-service to, the wider benefits of learning. Education does more than raise skills levels: it promotes active citizenship, has proven benefits for health, helps tackle poverty and social exclusion, and is a key part of neighbourhood renewal. Such education, harder perhaps to define and quantify, but just as important, is the proper job of good further and adult education.

A view from OECD

People working in further education, and especially principals, need no reminding that the overall performance of the UK in international league tables is extremely patchy. They have been so informed very frequently. It is of course a matter of great importance, and the issues bear repeating here, because this paper is for a wider audience, and the case for improvement needs constant emphasis.

At the Learning and Skills Development Agency summer conference in June 2003 a lucid and compelling presentation was made by Dr Barry McGaw, Director for Education in the Organisation for Economic Co-operation and Development (OECD). The work on education in OECD is concerned with making strategies for lifelong learning a reality. It includes work on approaches to making learning accessible in terms of pedagogy and location, the workforce skills demands of knowledge economies, and barriers to investment in lifelong learning. It develops quantitative indicators of education systems.

The work of OECD underlines Government concerns about the relatively poor performance of the UK in key areas, such as the number of 17-year-olds remaining in full-time education and training, and the large proportions of people in the workforce without qualifications. National performance for a good many years has been more likely to fall further behind that of other nations rather than to gain ground. For example, the UK went down from 13th to 22nd in its upper secondary completion rates over the past 30-40 years. At the same time, South Korea, with massive commitment to and investment in education, went from 24th to first and has had very high levels of economic growth to accompany its performance. The UK's upper secondary education completion rate is well behind those in many other OECD countries. Interestingly, any recent improvement in the UK position has been entirely attributable to increases in completion rates for women.

There is a direct correlation in the OECD's Growth Studies (the change in the economic growth rates) between human capital and the rate of economic growth.

> "The conclusion from the overall model …is that (human capital) has a significant impact across countries and that this impact is greatest in those countries that achieved the most substantial increase in human capital in the period between the mid-1980s and the mid-90s."

To underline the point:

> "it is clear that the average number of years of education completed in the working-age population will be increased only slowly by increasing participation rates in the current school-age population. The skills of the workforce could probably be increased more quickly and efficiently by training of adults."

There is a very clear policy indicator here for Britain, one which is now well understood, and one which is a key issue for colleges.

The OECD study also included calculations on the economic benefits gained by individuals who successfully complete tertiary education. The UK was second to the United States in rate of return from completion of higher secondary education, and had the highest rate of all OECD countries in rate of return from tertiary education. Whilst it can be argued that these rates of return stem in part at least from a more elitist system of higher education in the UK, and that the rate is likely to drop as we develop the projected higher levels of participation, the clear economic benefits of higher levels of qualification will remain. The arguments both for the nation and for individuals for economic growth through educational growth are compelling. (So, it might be argued, is the case for a requirement for individuals to contribute more to the costs of providing those qualifications, thus enabling state funding to benefit most those whose need is greatest. But that is not for here.)

In summary, the OECD work leads to the firm conclusion that both countries and individuals want more education, and the desire is well justified by the returns. Educational attainment matters for countries, because it leads to economic growth and to a high social rate of return. It matters to individuals because it gives a high personal rate of return and all the benefits that flow from it.

There is encouragement for the UK in the OECD Programme for International Student Assessment figures for 2001. In reading literacy, the UK shows up as a high-average performer, with its 15-year-olds ranked joint fourth among the OECD countries (Finland is top). The UK is also high-average in mathematical literacy at joint fifth (Japan top) and in scientific literacy third (Korea top). Rather less cause for satisfaction comes from some intriguing Johari window analyses, looking at mean performance, the spread of results, and social background. The UK comes out as a 'high quality low equity' country. "Students from disadvantaged backgrounds are much less well provided for by the education system in the UK than are such students in other high-performing countries like Finland, Korea, Japan, Canada and Ireland." This is no cause for great surprise: what ought to surprise us is the fact that we have allowed this situation to continue for so long. It has been a defining characteristic of our education system for very many years.

There is much food for thought in the OECD work, and it adds new urgency to what most educators have known for a long time. Bluntly, the education system has never served the needs of all of the people: there are millions in this country who have been failed by it: the rate of failure is scarcely changing: radical reform will be needed to produce radical change. We need to raise expectations and open opportunities. We need urgent reform of secondary education and curriculum, which has started but is not yet radical enough, and we need national strategies to provide, more quickly, for the many adults who have not completed the equivalent of upper secondary education. Dr McGaw again: "Alongside an expansion of provisions, there will need to be careful enhancement of the incentives for further education and training to ensure that increased supply is driven by an informed and motivated increase in demand. Clear qualification frameworks that grant recognition to competencies developed in ways that have currency in the labour market as well as general esteem can contribute to this enhancement of incentives."

Qualifications

There cannot be much doubt that present arrangements constitute a powerful disincentive. There is, and has been for a considerable amount of time, a serious problem with vocational qualifications in the British system. The issues have effect at all levels and at all ages: the current focus on the 14-19 curriculum is one very clear example of the importance and urgency of the need for reform, but it is far from the only one. The performance of FE colleges has been adversely affected since Incorporation by related issues: the lack of significant progress in the development of work-based learning is also partly a consequence of an unwieldy, inappropriate and inflexible system. There has been no attempt until very recently to create a coherent structure.

Earlier in this paper there has been reference to the essentially elitist nature of the education system, one which has resisted all attempts to make it more inclusive, more fit for the needs of the 20th Century, let alone the 21st Century. British class structures have shaped and preserved it: it has been a system designed to meet the needs of those looking for a university education, and it has paid too little attention to the majorities for which that was never an option. Our vocational routes have always been seen as second best, and do not communicate confidence, and even when attempts have been made to rectify the resultant problems, we revert to inappropriate academic assessment methodologies. General National Vocational Qualifications were forced into an A level mould. National Vocational Qualifications have offered pathways that were not available before, but have been too narrowly defined, measuring competence but largely ignoring underpinning knowledge. They have not been utilised by large parts of industry. The need for radical reform has become more and more urgent, and that of qualification systems and structures is critical.

It is the case that there is no trademark qualification in further education – unlike schools, with GCSE and A levels, and universities with degrees. It is estimated that there are as many as 20,000 different diplomas, certificates and other awards on offer in vocational education. There is little public understanding of their relative values against each other, or against so-called 'academic' qualifications. There are too many competing awarding bodies, each anxious to promote their own products: it has been impossible, or extremely difficult, for any tailoring of qualifications to meet the specific needs of the customers to take place. The ruling by the Further Education Funding Council (FEFC) that only full qualifications, successfully undertaken, were eligible for funding, very seriously distorted the performance of colleges at a critical time, and did little to serve the needs of learners. It also distorted perceptions of the performance of colleges by Ministers. It was a serious mistake from which we are still suffering, and the lessons of which we have been very slow to learn.

The system with which we work is inefficient, causing further problems for colleges and learners, and is extremely costly. The average college spends at least £250,000 each year on examination fees, the larger colleges much more. The aggregated sum may be as high as £150 million per year.

Inflexibility may be the worst of the problems. A rigidly centralised system controlled by the Qualifications and Curriculum Authority (QCA) – though it must be stated that the new Chief Executive recognises the urgency of a much faster approvals system – has delayed the introduction of new, better-designed qualifications, and has militated against learner-sensitive approaches to assessment. The seemingly inevitable British drift back to examinations as the only reliable – i.e. trustworthy – method of assessment goes on ensuring not only that people fail, but that they do not feel like trying again to succeed.

A key purpose of qualifications must be to motivate learners to achieve, to demonstrate their learning ability. Too much of our present system does that very imperfectly. Of course we also need to ensure standards, to measure comparability as well as individual success, and to aid labour mobility, but we are at risk of losing the learners in this, and of neglecting equality of opportunity as well as motivation.

There is reason to hope that progress is being made to secure a much more helpful system, in which the needs of learners, of employers, and ultimately the nation, will be much better met. It would appear that the damage that has been caused by past attitudes and practice is now better understood, and that there is evidence of a concerted effort to achieve lasting change and reform. The recent announcement by the Chief Executive of QCA that we are to have a unitised, credit-based system of vocational qualifications is a landmark statement, and it can have been made only with the active approval of the Department for Education and Skills (and indeed 10 Downing Street). It begs the question: why only vocational qualifications? But it is a long-awaited and highly significant step. If the structures to be put in place are thorough and consistent with the declared intention, then the movement towards reform of all our qualifications, A levels and all, will become irresistible. A baccalaureate style of qualification will surely follow.

The importance for adult learners, whatever their reasons for pursuing study, is great. A credit-based system will bring about a transformation in vocational qualifications and, we can hope, in attitudes towards assessment systems. The vision now is that

> "By 2007 modern qualifications will be tailored and quality assured to meet sector needs, and placed in unit-based credit frameworks. Adaptable assessment and funding arrangements will extend access and take-up, improve equality of opportunity and promote lifelong learning. This revitalised system will support employers, young people and adults by developing the skills of the workforce and improving international competitiveness."

This is taken from the report of the QCA/LSC/LSDA working party on vocational qualifications and credit-based system, now published on the QCA website.. If we achieve this transformation we make it possible to move from a supply-driven to a demand-led system with the potential for an exponential increase in opportunity. Since the LSC is engaged in this major policy development, we can hope that there is parallel work in train to ensure that funding methodologies will be in place to support the reform. In its Technical Document on 'Funding Adult Learning', the LSC cites the example of Access to Higher Education courses offered in FE colleges, the large majority of which are unit-based credit frameworks validated by Open College Networks. The methodologies already exist, and demonstrably work in the interests of learners, and of Government policy, in widening participation in both further and higher education. The consultation paper mentioned above recognises that a national credit framework would need a system of funding that reflected 'the flexible and incremental nature of engagement in learning'.

So we can hope to have in place within four years the unitised credit-based for vocational qualifications that QCA has announced, and a funding system that will support it. After waiting so long, four years may be thought to be acceptable – but it will be vital that there is a vigorous and concerted campaign to ensure that the significance of this momentous change is fully understood and properly anticipated. It has the potential to transform educational opportunity in this country. Colleges in particular will need to keep faith, to rediscover if necessary the real benefits of learner-centred curriculum design and teaching methods, and to ensure that they influence the debate about the funding support that will enable it to succeed. There is the chance to move from a system of qualifications that is rigid, highly centralised, slow, unresponsive, supply-driven, to one which can be learner-centred and demand-led. The qualifications framework, which according to the QCA's Chief Executive does not currently help the Government to achieve its objectives, can become flexible and supple, supportive of the design of curriculum that will meet needs. But we will have to keep pushing, and further and adult educators will need to bring their collective influence to bear.

FE/HE

There is now more higher education work taking place in further education than there was in the whole of the HE system at the time of the Robbins Report (1963). The figure, now around 12 per cent, has grown considerably since Incorporation which, among other things, removed the right of veto operated by Higher Education Institutions (HEIs) sitting on the Regional Advisory Councils, which exercised a measure of control over the FE curriculum. The Councils were substantially funded by the Local Education Authorities (LEAs) which, when they relinquished their responsibility for the colleges, not unnaturally declined to go on doing so.

Colleges were then freed up to expand or develop their offer, whether through growth in provision of professional courses, by programmes validated or franchised by partner universities, or by securing funding for Higher National Diploma and Certificate courses. The colleges which had historically received some funding from the then University Grants Committee were in a particularly strong position to achieve growth. At the same time, of course, HE itself was expanding rapidly, with the creation of the new (ex-Polytechnic) universities which all had their roots in further education, and funding for growth throughout the system. It is worth noting, however, that in most HE policy documents part-time and adult students are almost entirely invisible.

In fact, the number of adult students in HE is now larger than the number of 18-21-year-olds. However, the proportions engaged in HE in Britain are still well below those in many competitor nations, and in addition the social class gap in entry to higher education is unacceptably wide. Numbers of those entering from lower-income families have risen, but the proportion has not. There is massive waste of potential, both among young people and adults, and while the Government's somewhat wavering target of 50 per cent of 18-30-year-olds to benefit from higher education deserves strong support, the DfES has not yet been convincing about those in older age brackets. Unless there is clear policy to redress the imbalance, we will go on failing individuals and society as a whole and creating new divisions, damaging commendable effort elsewhere. We need to identify and implement the strategies that will give us a universal higher education system.

Any discussion about the place of further education colleges within the higher education system, and indeed about adult students in HE, is about the changing nature of higher education. Universities have not been noted for their willingness to change, though no doubt would argue that they have transformed themselves in recent years, and there are honourable exceptions. It would be absurd to suggest that a system which has moved from one which catered for less than 5 per cent of the school-leaving population only 40 years ago to its present 35 per cent + has not had to adapt. But some, very clearly, have adapted much more than others.

It remains the case that very many aspects of university education are seen in much the same terms as would have applied before the last great market-driven expansion of the early 1990s. As NIACE put it in its response to the White Paper in 2003:

> "Higher education is perceived in the Paper as essentially similar in composition and experience to the system with which many of the present generation of policy makers grew up."

The concept of the three-year full-time degree offered largely to school-leavers or school-leavers+1 (the gap year having become fashionable) still drives the thinking. In fact, in 2001/2002 54 per cent of students in HE were over 21, including 29 per cent of those studying full-time. (Ninety-two per cent of all part-time students in HE were over 21.) Furthermore, the distinction between full-time and part-time is increasingly blurred – this is very much the case in further education – as students seek paid employment to help support them. In this respect there is little difference between HE and FE students.

There is widespread agreement that an advanced 21st Century economy needs very high levels of qualifications and learning capacity in its workforce and among its citizens. There is agreement too that the implied system of universal higher education will – and should – look fundamentally different from the present system. It will need to be much more learner-focused, provide high quality and diverse learning support, and be more responsive and adaptable in its delivery.

The FE contribution

Further education colleges are crucial to such a system, but there will need to be some fundamental changes in thinking, both at Government and at institutional level, if they are to fulfil this role. It is increasingly difficult, in an era of policy priorities and target-driven funding, to maintain all the aspects of the mission which was once seen as FE's greatest strength, its willingness to provide for the whole of its community, to respond to the needs of learners flexibly and adaptively, to respond to opportunity. The priorities of current Government policy are touched on elsewhere, but the interests of adult learners with the capability, the desire and the will to study in higher education need to be safeguarded and promoted, and FE colleges need to be encouraged and funded to see that as one of their key tasks. The case is not being made strongly enough at the present time, not by Government, not by the colleges and their organisations, and certainly not by the universities.

FE colleges have a long history of effective work with non-traditional learners, and equally with those returning to education after a period, sometimes long, away from it. Access to HE courses in FE have been instrumental in bringing thousands of students into HE who would not have had such opportunity otherwise. Insufficient attention has been paid to this success and the curriculum design and the pedagogic methods which sustain it. Admittedly retention rates have suffered, principally because mature part-time learners without financial support could not afford to remain as students. Support systems in FE colleges are usually good, and the success rate of those students who manage to steer their way round all the hurdles is high.

As a recent HEFCE publication (*Supporting higher education in further education colleges*, 2003) noted, colleges operate in a world of contradictions. Funding, quality assurance systems and government policy are not designed to ease the task of developing HE provision, and often appear to hinder it. This same publication from HEFCE lists 14 strengths of colleges in offering HE, ranging from 'regular access to supportive and friendly staff' to 'flexible timetabling', 'plenty of teaching support' to 'relevant curricula for new kinds of learners'. The document also reports that "the majority of Quality Assurance Agency subject reviews of HE in FE have identified far more strengths than weaknesses."

The attributed strengths and distinctiveness of HE in FE, as evidenced in the HEFCE publication, might be regarded as exactly the same strengths which good FE colleges bring to bear in all of their work with adults. It would be facile to claim that all such work is uniformly good, but the quality of student care, of teaching support, of most of the teaching and – where possible – the curriculum design and development, is generally high and is regarded as so by learners. The quality of the learning experience matters to most FE staff: they want to help learners to learn. This is especially so where the motivation of the learners is high, as with almost all adult learners. This is why HE in FE works, and why it needs to be encouraged and utilised more.

Models of association

There are some interesting models of association developing in different parts of the country, and it is in partnerships that most progress will be made. The best of these will be partnerships of equals, in which the strengths of the partners are properly understood and valued. Staffordshire University made a bold decision some years ago, focusing all of its partnership work on a defined geographical area and its regional colleges, even at the expense of good relationships with colleges further afield.

Warwick had the same kind of arrangement in place much earlier, when the 2 + 2 model was developed with partner colleges in Warwickshire, Coventry and Solihull. The Warwickshire Community University was one of the first of its kind, but its demise – admittedly largely through the cost pressures on the 2 + 2 model – is instructive, in that it did not survive the departure from the university of its strongest proponents. Russell Group status inevitably was a higher priority.

There are now many models, some of them (Humber Consortium and Greater Manchester, for example) led by FE institutions. Some others have every appearance of being take-overs, and there is a strong danger of the FE focus and distinctive strength being lost. The Suffolk College / University of East Anglia Partnership appears to be based on real equality and mutual respect, with UEA acting as the sole validating institution, but with joint academic planning and strong formal and informal links.

Collaboration, whether through formally constituted partnerships and consortia, or more *ad hoc* groupings, will remain the principal and necessary route through which HE in FE will grow. The provision of foundation degrees is one key area for further development: they are much more likely to be based in a college where the validating university has pre-existing arrangements. Whether this will be enough to ensure the kind of growth in foundation degrees that is needed is debatable, because the number of colleges in the appropriate kind of partnerships is a minority. Other stimulus may be needed if foundation degrees are to become an important feature of HE expansion, such as the active participation of employers, or the creation of a body equivalent to the old Council for National Academic Awards to provide validation for approved programmes.

Foundation degrees may become a valuable means of providing greater access, and of greater vocational content in the curriculum, but they may also become another failed initiative, like Diplomas in Higher Education. This is one of the areas where a major shift in thinking is required: foundation degrees will be more successful if a greater degree of responsibility for their development is given to FE. They are not yet, and will probably never be, sufficiently high on the agenda of most universities. We need either a new independent awarding body, or we need new models of association between colleges and partner universities. These must not be based on the usual hierarchical arrangements: the colleges need to be seen as equal and strategic partners, bringing their own essential strengths.

There is an important opportunity here, but one which will very easily be lost if not grasped. History does not support an assumption that the kind of changes that are necessary will be forthcoming through the usual modest incremental adjustments which leave the architecture largely unaltered. The initiative must be taken – by Government or by HEFCE – to create a new structure, ideally not just for the proper development of foundation degrees but as part of a movement towards a new tertiary system.

In the meantime, there is need for much more research into the different kinds of arrangements that now exist between FE and HE institutions, with the express purpose of ensuring that opportunity for adult students is extended. Beyond that, we need to secure a consensus on the need for, and identify the practical means of moving towards, a robust system of universal tertiary / higher education.

The American model, in this if not in everything, has much to commend it. The kind of relationship which exists between the community colleges and the state universities, built on an effective and fully-accepted system of credit assessment and accumulation, makes for smooth – even automatic – arrangements for transition and progression, and builds on the broad and egalitarian access mission of the colleges. We have the chance to grow something similar and equally effective here, with the added dimension of the stronger vocational traditions of our colleges. But there are formidable barriers, of which elitism and the stultifying effects of social class in our society are perhaps the greatest.

The argument of this paper is that the work of the further education colleges, with due regard for the importance of their contribution to more successful outcomes in 14-19 education, and their vital work in improvements of levels of basic skills, is best seen as part of a tertiary system. Such a system, in which full and just emphasis is given to the need of adult learners at all stages of their lives, would transform our perceptions of HE, the opportunities available to individuals, and the social and economic health of the country. In this, as with qualifications, as with funding methodologies, as with social inclusion, we need a Big Bang. Without it, inertia is likely to win.

(One anecdote, unattributable but true, of a comment from a university admissions tutor to an FE Access lecturer: 'Are you sending us any more charity cases this year?')

The Skills Strategy

The Skills Strategy White Paper (*21st Century Skills: Realising our Potential*) is good news.

It is to the credit of the Government that it has recognised so clearly that there is a serious skills deficit, and that it is damaging growth and productivity in the economy. Figures for Gross Domestic Product (GDP) per worker make the latter fact very clear. If the index of productivity stands at 100 for the UK, it is at 112 in Germany, 117 in France, and 138 in the US. GDP per hour worked, again on the same base, gives US 129, and both France and Germany 132. This kind of gap in productivity is clearly unsustainable for very long.

So we need higher levels of skill and qualification in the workforce and we need to plan for and achieve considerable improvement among existing workers as well as those preparing to enter it. Both industry and individuals must have access to and support in achieving the skills that they need. Hence the Skills Strategy.

National problems are well documented for young people. Far too many complete initial education unprepared for the labour market and with inadequate qualifications: too many leave full-time education, or indeed any kind of education, too early. Vocational routes are held in lower esteem than 'academic' pathways, whether for progression to HE or to employment: there is continuing shortfall in the required levels of both core and specific skills. The proposals in *14-19: Opportunity and Excellence* are intended to address all of these areas of weakness, but some observers are disappointed that it seems to be intended that 'new' curriculum structures may be substantially based on existing ones. ("Any new award should be based around existing national qualifications such as GCSEs, A levels and Modern Apprenticeships.") More radical solutions to a very long-standing and damaging problem will be needed: a bolder approach in this area would bring short-term problems over perceptions, but is likely to have much greater chance of long-term success.

Our present system of full-time education reinforces inequality, as the OECD evidence confirms, and it will not be changed if most of the present architecture is left in place. When we have, as confirmed in the White Paper, a unitised, credit-based system of vocational qualifications – and this is the best news we have had in many years in this sphere – we must ensure that there is strong promotion of its advantages to all, and a clear understanding of the benefits it will bring. The curriculum, and the way in which it is assessed (and taught) is the key to better skills development for young people.

As far as those who are already in the workforce are concerned the issues are not dissimilar. They are, after all, the product of the same system that we know needs urgent reform. One third of those now in work are not qualified to level 2 and there are seven million adults without adequate literacy and numeracy. The majority of those not now in any form of formal learning have no wish to return to it, and those with low skills or none at all are much less likely to be receiving training in employment. Graduates are five times more likely to be receiving training than the unqualified.

The deep seated causes of these problems lie in the elitist nature of the system which, despite all the reviews and commissions, all the schemes and attempted reforms, remains much too narrow and much too academic. The perceived lack of responsiveness on the supply side, the paucity of meaningful employer engagement, the low value attached to vocational education, the acceptance of the low skills equilibrium, the lukewarm attitude towards foundation degrees, are all rooted deep in our educational culture.

This White Paper attempts substantial change. Although it is to be regretted that the commitment to entitlement to all for a level 3 qualification has been dropped – this was one of Helena Kennedy's strongest recommendations – there is much to cheer, and much that should be welcomed by the FE sector. There is free entitlement to a first level 2 qualification for adults, with a maintenance grant of £30 to help learners study full-time. However, the case for support for those with no choice but to study part-time is not met, and this will limit the impact of the changes. There is explicit ring-fencing of funding to support free training to level 3 in key skills shortage areas. There is the promised reform of vocational qualifications, the lifting of the age cap on Modern Apprenticeships – first step to MAs for adults. There is strong recognition of the importance of Basic Skills, with the inclusion of ICT as the third of them: there is a continued commitment to those strategies which promote social inclusion. The Paper is sensible too on the importance of active promotion of these reforms, and of high quality Information and Guidance. It seeks to extend the excellent work which goes on under the Union Learning Fund, and gives statutory recognition to union learning representatives.

There is a very clear commitment to the safeguarding of a wide range of learning for adults, for culture, leisure, community and personal fulfilment. The fears of many adult educators will have been allayed by paragraphs 41 and 42 of Chapter 4. There is perhaps a stronger recognition here than ever before of the social benefits of learning.

Funds are guaranteed in LSC budgets for such learning, and minimum figures are set. This guarantee, however, appears not to include such work undertaken by colleges. This may well have unfortunate and perhaps unintended effects, with a possible narrowing of the adult curriculum in areas where colleges are the main providers.

This distinction would seem anomalous, but raises the fear that there is a wish to narrow the role of the colleges. It reinforces the high desirability of joint approaches between FE and NIACE in the defence of all aspects of adult education.

There are important structural proposals in the White Paper. A national Skills Alliance will bring together DTI with DfES, with the LSC, Confederation for British Industry, the Trades Union Congress and the Sector Skills Council, to ensure effective coordination. Regionally, led by the Regional Development Agencies, local LSCs, Job Centre Plus, Sector Skills Councils and Business Link will seek to effect similar coordination.

The Foreword to the White Paper talks of the need for sustained effort over the long term to put right the deficiencies of the past, and of five key areas, described in five paragraphs. The first is about employers' needs, second about raising ambition, third about motivation and support, and the fifth about joined-up government. The fourth:

> 'We must make colleges and training providers more responsive to employers' and learners' needs, reaching out to more businesses and more people, and providing training in ways that suit them. Creating a truly-demand-led approach means reforming qualifications, reforming the way we fund colleges, and reforming the way we deliver training.'

There is a clear challenge here to colleges, but equally a great opportunity. The reform of qualifications, long overdue, can prove the catalyst for a major leap forward, but it requires colleges to place greater focus than most have in recent years on curriculum and effective teaching and learning.

FE and ACL

The recent Review of Adult and Community Learning conducted by the Birmingham and Solihull LSC had to start its work by deciding what it sought to review. What is ACL? Is it that work funded through LEAs, out of the ACL fund? Does it include Schedule 2 as well as non-Schedule 2 in the old FEFC definitions? Do colleges directly funded by LSC do ACL, or just adult learning? Is the term confined to learning delivered through outreach provision? Is it that which is non-accredited?

The DfES seems to know. The Skills Strategy White Paper makes the promise that there will be a protected fund for 'leisure, culture and community learning'. It will perhaps be some time before we know how big this fund will be, quite which work qualifies for it, and how it will be dispensed. It is unlikely that all of the vagaries will be removed. It appears that this protected fund will not be applicable to work undertaken by colleges.

The Birmingham and Solihull answer was a pragmatic one. ACL was defined as those activities engaging adults in:

- first-rung provision taking place on an institutional or an outreach basis organised by colleges, voluntary and community organisations or by the LEAs, with encouragement to progress to higher level vocational or academic provision.
- non-vocational programmes organised by the colleges, voluntary or community organisations or by the LEAs.
- Basic Skills
- ESOL
- Basic ICT

This works well enough, though it begs a number of questions, but once agreed had the virtue of pre-empting further discussion. For interest, there were 185,000 learners engaged in provision under these definitions in Birmingham and Solihull in 2000/2001, of which 104,000 were over 19. The research conducted for the Review identified no fewer than 900 voluntary and community sector organisations involved in delivering and/or signposting learning. The area of learning involving most students was ICT, followed by foundation programmes including basic skills. Together these accounted for 43 per cent of adult enrolments. (Which means that something of the order of 56,000 were following other programmes within this definition. It would be interesting to compare that number, as a proportion of total population, with other areas.) Birmingham has a long-established and thriving Adult Education Service with around 35,000 learners. Around half of them are on 'leisure' courses, and the other half on what we would once have described as Schedule 2. The city also has 10 FE colleges, all of which offer varying amounts of adult and community provision, some of them very substantial amounts.

What is important here is to avoid getting bogged down in definitions, and at all costs to avoid turf wars. The real subject is adult education in all its forms. The work that goes on in communities, through outreach, is a vital part of educational opportunity for adults. So is leisure and culture-orientated provision, and it matters little who provides it.

The work in the community, and the work in the voluntary sector, is a crucial part of the landscape of change. If, as we know to be the case, many thousands of people have been rejected by our education systems, have been failed by structures and methods that were not designed for them, then the task of reaching them requires very special skills and approaches. Colleges themselves rarely have resources to do all that is necessary, though there is excellent work in some. We need to build climbing frames of opportunity, with access at every level and help wherever it is required. ACL works with disaffected young people, offenders, refugees, single parents, and many who would not normally find their way to colleges. Much of it is first-step provision, and without it there could be no progression for such learners.

It is therefore a wholly legitimate area for the new Skills Strategy, and credit is due to those who have worked hard to present the case to Government. Family learning, family literacy and numeracy, community art, can and do start learners on a path that leads to qualified employment, honours degrees, healthy and fulfilling lives. ACL is a vital part of the climbing frame.

We need to ensure that progression routes are always open and that well-informed and independent advice is available. Close working relationships between those working in ACL and those providing for adults in colleges are necessary, and need to be facilitated and resourced. Enlightened local LSCs will do this, and NIACE can advise on best practice. Attention needs to be focused on the key requirements of Adult and Community Learning to engage new learners, ensure there are opportunities for clear progression into further and, where appropriate, accredited learning, and seek to remove barriers to participation. This is again core work for FE. It will often be best developed and delivered in partnerships with ACL providers.

Conclusions

As has been acknowledged throughout this paper, the Government is deserving of credit for what it is trying to achieve. All of the recent policy initiatives are necessary attempts to solve the long-standing problems of the national system. There is evidence of a coherent strategy for change and improvement: the ambition is for a society which is both fair and successful. And, as paymasters, Ministers are in charge, and they are increasing the level of resource.

No Government, however, has demonstrated an intuitive or even a detailed understanding of what the further education system does. The sector is at risk of being forced into a narrow definition of its contribution, and of seeing some of its greatest strengths atrophy. FE can and should utilise its experience and resources to help revitalise the 14-19 curriculum, and it must play a full part in the necessary efforts to improve skills and qualifications of those in the workforce and those preparing to enter it. It will be grateful for some of the opportunities that the Skills Strategy presents. But it should not allow itself to be forced away from some of the things it does best.

The sector overall may be weaker than at any time since Incorporation. Financial issues still dog a large minority of colleges, and some of the freedoms that came with FEFC have been lost. But not all colleges are equal, and there are very many, especially the large urban colleges, which deserve the right to determine their own missions and priorities: by no means to ignore Government requirements, but to go on developing their core strengths. Many of those strengths relate to the work that colleges do with adult students, whether in basic skills, vocational and professional qualifications, higher education – and in adult and community programmes.

We are too much driven by targets and delivery, at the expense of important educational considerations. Colleges are taken to task for retention rates that are the subject of envy in American institutions, improvable though ours are. The LSC has been given what we will come to see as an impossible task: it is a planning body without the real capacity to plan, dealing as it does in each or most of its 47 branches with hundreds of tiny providers. It rearranges learner support funds without real understanding of the consequences, in pursuit of arbitrary targets. It measures performance (as does Ofsted) by the wrong criteria. Sooner or later it will be succeeded by new regional structures in which economic planning, skills development, sector skills councils, and possibly even higher education will be coordinated.

In the meantime, good colleges need to represent themselves and their constituencies much more vigorously. They should fight the cause for all their learners, the great majority of whom are, as we have seen, adults. And they should form alliances, to influence more vigorously Government perceptions and policies. They are the primary education providers for their whole communities, and this role is vital to most of what the Government is trying to do. The work-based strand, and improved levels of skills are essential, and colleges should be arguing their case to strengthen their capacity to play a major part in it.

But general further education, and adult education, are important too, and the role of the FE colleges, constituting the only grouping of organisations which operates in this field on a national basis, is to defend it, and work with others with the same commitment. The Association for Colleges, under new leadership, might respond to the challenge. FE needs to represent itself, taking a vigorous role in all of the new initiatives but refusing to compromise with its core values. It also needs to work much more closely than most of it has done hitherto with NIACE, which shares those same values, and which has a key role to play. Further, there is an important policy directive for NIACE here. It needs to make vigorous effort to raise its profile among the FE colleges and those who shape policy relevant to their work. As this paper has attempted to demonstrate, the very large majority of what takes place in general FE colleges (and in specialist colleges of art, of agriculture, and so on) is about the education of adults. It is therefore unquestionably the business of NIACE – as is, of course, the promotion of the interests of adult learners in HE. NIACE is a highly successful organisation, with great sense of its values and its purpose. It needs to ensure that it is clear to everyone that FE is a central part of its work and its mission.

Policy recommendations

- The stated commitment to a credit framework for adult learners, together with the parallel reform of qualifications, needs to be sustained, adequately resourced and supported, and progressed as a matter of urgency.

- Such a framework will provide a tool to aid the design of more flexible curriculum provision that is responsive to the demands of individuals and employers. The colleges of further education must be encouraged, in building on their existing expertise, to expand their capacity to utilise this crucial opportunity to full advantage.

- The anticipated reforms of the 14-19 curriculum are crucial to the long-term success of the Skills Strategy and to the necessary improvements in participation and achievement of young adults. They will need to be radical in design and decisively and courageously implemented.

- In the longer term it will be necessary to seek the implementation of a unified framework of qualifications, in order to promote and facilitate optimum opportunity for progression and to promote the development of a lifelong learning culture. We will need aligned qualifications structures if we are to avoid disjuncture. Planning for such a system should now be put in hand.

  The lead responsibility for the reform of the qualifications system rests with DfES and QCA, working with appropriate awarding bodies. Key partners are the LSC and the providers, notably the colleges.

- The contribution made by further education colleges to the expansion of opportunity in higher education needs to be celebrated, further encouraged and systematically monitored and developed. The most successful models of association between further and higher education institutions should be identified and appropriately promoted.

- If foundation degrees are to fulfil the hopes placed in them, and create a vigorous and vocational first phase of higher education, more of their development should be entrusted to those colleges of further education which have successfully demonstrated their capacity in higher education. DfES and HEFCE should investigate appropriate mechanisms to facilitate such a policy shift. The college contribution must be seen as mainstream, not peripheral.

  Lead responsibilities: DfES and HEFCE.

- The role of successful colleges and further education provision in promoting social inclusivity and an equitable, informed and healthy society needs more positive recognition and encouragement, and should be made a key component in government policy.

- The colleges themselves, and their organisations, need to build and assert their confidence in their role and their distinctive vision. Their voices, collectively and individually, need to be heard more frequently in the development and influencing of policy and in the invigoration of their local communities and of educational strategies. The turbulences and traumas of the last ten years must be made irrelevant.

  Lead responsibility: DfES, the colleges and their organisations.

● Work-based learning is an essential part of national strategies, but is not yet effectively and sufficiently part of national planning. The best models of collaboration between further education providers and employers, including those supported by the Trades Unions Learning Fund need to be identified and promulgated. This proposal could become part of the work of the Skills Alliance, with consequent recommendations.

Lead responsibility: LSC (nationally and locally), CBI, TUC, the colleges.

● The importance of non-accredited learning in the development of the increased well-being of British society, and the achievement of higher measures of success in economic, social and personal terms, needs to be ringingly affirmed, actively promoted, and, where necessary, supportively resourced.

Lead responsibility: NIACE; key partners: the colleges and their organisations.

● To help steer and monitor progress towards all of the above there is need for an active working alliance of those organisations and institutions committed to the achievement of them. There is a key role for NIACE in the building of such an alliance.

● In order to fulfil its role and contribute fully to the policies recommended above, NIACE should:

   ● Strengthen its capacity in FE
   ● Promote the advantages of membership to colleges
   ● Institute regular contact with the colleges
   ● Plan and deliver regular conferences which are clearly relevant to FE ambitions and concerns
   ● Take a lead role in the formation of alliances and partnerships with organisations active in FE and adult learning.
   ● Consider instituting new publications aimed at the FE sector
   ● Play an active and visible role in advocacy for adult learners in FE
   ● Seek opportunity to stimulate, contribute to and encourage participation in active debate on FE policy issues.

Lead responsibility: NIACE and its partners.

Other new **NIACE** policy discussion papers

Adult Learners in a Brave New World – Lifelong learning policy and structural changes since 1997, Leisha Fullick, 2004, ISBN 1 86201 178 8

Testing testing 1 2 3: Assessment in adult literacy, language and numeracy, Peter Lavender, Jay Derrick and Barry Brooks, 2004, ISBN 1 86201 193 1

Learning's Not a Crime: Education and training for offenders and ex-offenders in the Community, Tony Uden, 2004, ISBN 1 86201 207 5